EARTHFORMS

RIVERS

By Martha London

Consultant: Beth Gambro
Reading Specialist, Yorkville, Illinois

Minneapolis, Minnesota

Teaching Tips

Before Reading
- Look at the cover of the book. Discuss the picture and the title.
- Ask readers to brainstorm a list of what they already know about rivers. What can they expect to see in the book?
- Go on a picture walk, looking through the pictures to discuss vocabulary and make predictions about the text.

During Reading
- Read for purpose. Encourage readers to think about characteristics of rivers.
- Ask readers to look for the details of the book. How are rivers made?
- If readers encounter an unknown word, ask them to look at the sounds in the word. Then, ask them to look at the rest of the page. Are there any clues to help them understand?

After Reading
- Encourage readers to pick a buddy and reread the book together.
- Ask readers to name two places river water can come from. Find the pages that tell about these things.
- Ask readers to write or draw something they learned about rivers.

Credits

Cover and title page, © benedek/iStock; 3, © Elis Cora/iStock; 5, © Mark Lee/iStock; 7, © Alexis Gonzalez/iStock; 8–9, © Bkamprath/iStock; 11, © Aleksandra Tokarz/iStock; 13, © Justinreznick/iStock; 14–15, © Bim/iStock; 16–17, © miharing/iStock; 18–19, © blueringmedia/iStock; 21, © FatCamera/iStock; 22T, © undefined undefined/iStock; 22M, © pingebot/Shutterstock; 22B, © alexerich/iStock; 23TL, © Bartfett/iStock; 23TM, © ThomasVogel/iStock; 23TR, © shaunl/iStock; 23BL, © Bahadir Eroglu/iStock; 23BR, © JaySi/iStock.

See BearportPublishing.com for our statement on Generative AI Usage.

Library of Congress Cataloging-in-Publication Data

Names: London, Martha, author.
Title: Rivers / by Martha London ; Consultant: Beth Gambro, Reading Specialist, Yorkville Illinois.
Description: Bearcub books. | Minneapolis, Minnesota : Bearport Publishing Company, [2025] | Series: Earthforms | Includes bibliographical references and index.
Identifiers: LCCN 2024023210 (print) | LCCN 2024023211 (ebook) | ISBN 9798892326254 (library binding) | ISBN 9798892326650 (paperback) | ISBN 9798892327053 (ebook)
Subjects: LCSH: Rivers--Juvenile literature. | Nile River--Juvenile literature.
Classification: LCC GB1203.8 .L64 2025 (print) | LCC GB1203.8 (ebook) |
DDC 551.48/3--dc23/eng/20240601
LC record available at https://lccn.loc.gov/2024023210
LC ebook record available at https://lccn.loc.gov/2024023211

Copyright © 2025 Bearport Publishing Company. All rights reserved. No part of this publication may be reproduced in whole or in part, stored in any retrieval system, or transmitted in any form or by any means, electronic, mechanical, photocopying, recording, or otherwise, without written permission from the publisher.

For more information, write to Bearport Publishing, 5357 Penn Avenue South, Minneapolis, MN 55419.

Contents

Go with the Flow 4

Nile River 22
Glossary 23
Index 24
Read More 24
Learn More Online 24
About the Author 24

Go with the Flow

Water flows down the river.

Sticks and leaves float by.

Water splashes around rocks.

Blub, blub, blub.

What is a river?

A river is a **flowing** body of water.

Some rivers are wide and slow.

Others are small and have fast water.

River water can come from many places.

Some water comes from melting snow on mountains.

Other water comes out of lakes.

Rivers are always changing. A river can **flood** with lots of rain.

When there is no rain, rivers get smaller.

Some rivers even dry up.

Rivers can also change the land.

Fast water moves dirt and rocks.

The water makes a new **path** for the river.

14

Over time, a river carries away more and more dirt. It cuts deeper into the land.

After a long time, this can form a deep **canyon**.

Rivers give plants water to grow. Many animals live in rivers. Trout lay eggs in cold river water.

People need rivers, too. We use rivers to make **energy.** Flowing water turns wheels. This makes power for cities.

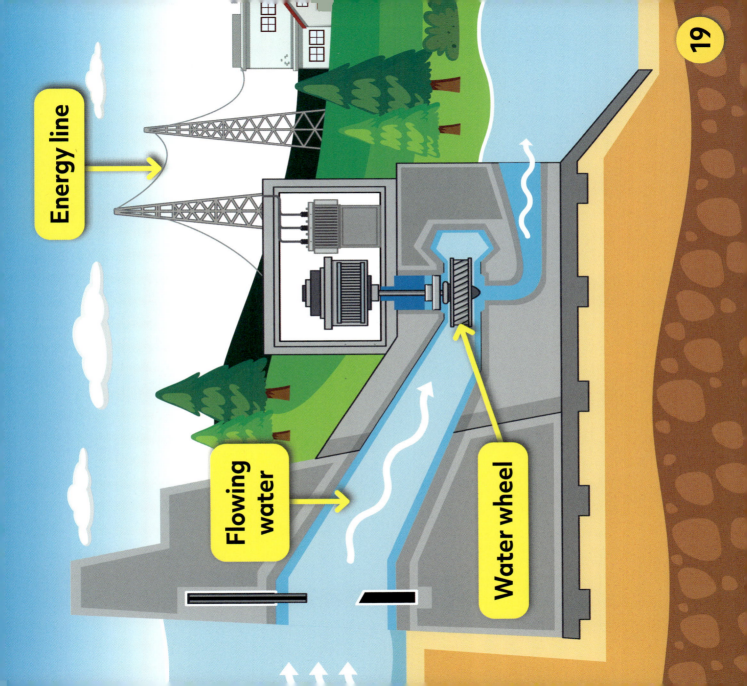

People have fun on rivers. They ride in boats and go fishing.

Do you have a river near you?

Nile River

The Nile River is one of the longest rivers in the world.

The Nile River flows through 11 countries.

Nile River
AFRICA

It is one of the only rivers that flows south to north.

Egyptians have farmed along the Nile for thousands of years.

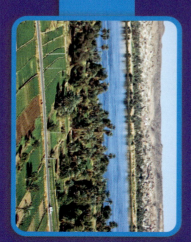

Glossary

flood to cover land with water

energy power that makes things work

canyon a deep cut in the ground

path the course along which something moves

flowing moving from one place to another

Index

canyon 14
energy 18–19
flood 10
lakes 8
land 12, 14
mountains 8
rain 10
rocks 4, 12

Read More

Andrews, Elizabeth. *Freshwater Biome (Beautiful Biomes).* Minneapolis: ABDO, 2022.

Berne, Emma Carlson. *Underwater Plants (A Watery World).* Minneapolis: Bearport, 2025.

Learn More Online

1. Go to **FactSurfer.com** or scan the QR code below.
2. Enter "**Earthforms Lakes**" into the search box.
3. Click on the cover of this book to see a list of websites.

About the Author

Martha London lives in Minnesota. She loves spending time outside.